The Smart Marketer's Guide to Google AdWords

By Noa Eshed and Uri Bishansky

Copyright

Cover design by: Marijo Šarić

ISBN-13: 978-1532750984

ISBN-10: 1532750986

Contents

Foreword

On one night in 1999, a bit before humanity entered the 21st century, my good friend Ami from New York called me. Ami told me he hadn't slept the night before. "I found an amazing toy. You have to try it. Listen, do you know Google? The search engine? they released something to the web. You can play around with it on your own. You can define search terms and in real time, whoever searches for those terms will find you from anywhere in the world. You define how much you want pay. It's cents!" I entered Google and of course I immediately fell in love. I created a table of words, I saw search results. I felt like I was programming the engine of the world.

The next morning, I approached the marketing team of our company. In those times, a very small percentage of our millions of dollars' global media budget was designated to the web, and was mostly targeting Alta Vista and Yahoo, the dominators of web search back then. I excitedly presented the new Google innovation and received unimpressed responses. "who knows Google? Who knows if this will work?" OK, I couldn't pass on this game so I announced I personally plan on continuing to manage the company Google search campaign I initiated, and that they could proceed taking care of all other marketing aspects.

It so happened that for almost a year, much before half of Israel's best marketers became online marketing experts, I was spending my nights searching, buying keywords and even optimizing search results in my new toy. Today, everybody is clear on who Google are. Within a decade, the marketing world went through a revolution which changed the entire world.

In 2008, our company Aladdin, with a revenue cycle of over 150 million USD per year, 600 employees and 10 worldwide branches, had already invested close to 10 million USD a year in online marketing.

My interest in online marketing proceeds to this day, when I first read Noa and Uri's book, I was filled with joy and longing. I felt a strong will to start another company, just so that I could market it online. Only those who tried this themselves can understand this feeling, but this time there is a guide. Noa and Uri did an excellent job writing this guide. This book is full of pages of joy and expertise. This book is a must for anybody who ever thought of marketing online. It is so delighting I'm actually thinking of inventing a new product, just so that I can market it properly.

Even if you are already Google AdWords experts, don't miss out on this wonderful book.

Yanki Margalit

Founder and former CEO of Aladdin Knowledge Systems, and Social Entrepreneur.

Introduction

The aim of this book is to provide marketers with a detailed and easy to understand explanation on how to create, measure and scale a Google AdWords campaign. We suggest that even if you are working with an agency, you invest a few hours to understanding the basics.

On a grand strategic level, this book will help you become a better marketer, focusing on smartly channeling your marketing efforts to platforms where you can track your progress and success.

Years of experience as Google Partners, managing businesses and campaigns worth millions of dollars have resulted in us understanding how to get the most out of paid advertising on Google AdWords. This book will cover the core do's and don'ts we have learned.

We will teach you how to:

- Setup successful campaigns all by yourself.

- Manage other people effectively in setting up and managing campaigns.

- Track every dollar spent and the impact it had on customers, sales and loyalty.

- Understand what exactly is working for you and what isn't.

- Generate a positive return on investment (ROI).

We will be largely focusing on two types of AdWords Campaigns in this book, i.e., – Search and Display Campaigns.

We hope you find this book as useful as we aim for it to be, getting your brain juices flowing and saving you time and money.

Good luck and we hope you're ready for your successful journey ahead!

Chapter 1: Setting the Stage - Online Advertising

"A man who stops advertising to save money is like a man who stops a clock to save time" Henry Ford.

Online advertising can sometimes seem overwhelming. Around the clock, prospective customers are looking up information on search engines and blogs, emailing, watching videos and consuming endless content online. Within this clutter, how can you make sure you place the right message, at the right time, to the right people? Let us begin by setting the stage.

Online Advertising can be largely divided into Search Engine Marketing (SEM), Display advertising, Video advertising and Inbound Sponsored Content Promotion:

- SEM is an online marketing initiative whereby traffic is driven to a website organically (using Search Engine Optimization (SEO) techniques) or by paid advertisements. Paid search advertising is a means of advertising where text and product ads are displayed along with paid Search Engine Result Pages (SERPS) related to matching key search terms (keywords).

- Display advertising incorporates banner/video advertisements across content websites.

- Video advertising uses text, banner and video ads across YouTube or other video platforms.

- Sponsored Content Promotion is a method of generating website traffic using platforms such as Taboola or Outbrain to display contextual recommended sponsored links.

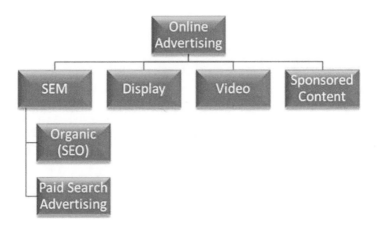

There are many digital advertising tools and techniques available besides Google AdWords, including advertising networks such as Bing ads, Facebook ads, Twitter ads, LinkedIn ads and many more. We will focus on Google AdWords – Google's advertising networks as Google is the world's largest online advertising platform aggregating about 83% of the world's advertising inventory or advertising space on websites across the world.

Google's Advertising Networks – Search and Display

The Googles AdWords Networks consists of Google Search Network (GSN) and Google Display Network (GDN). You can choose where your ads will appear on these networks. GSN includes Google Search and a host of Search Partners like AOL. It also includes other Google properties like Google Maps, Google Shopping (previously known as Google Product Listing Ads – PLAs), YouTube, and other Google Sites. GSN will enable you to advertise the products and services you're offering and puts you in front of customers who are interested in the kind of products or services you are offering.

The GDN aggregates more than a million websites including Google Sites and properties like YouTube, Blogger, Gmail, Google Partner Websites, and mobile apps. GDN enables you to place a variety of ad formats in front of people who are browsing the internet and target people who are consuming content that is related to your products/services. Therefore, even if they don't specifically access your website or content, they will be able to find you through other outlets as well.

Before proceeding to advertising on Google AdWords you will first need to know exactly who your prospective target customers are. We will discuss this in the next chapter.

Chapter 2: Understanding Your Customer

When implementing a digital campaign, the first things you have to understand are your current and prospective customers' needs, behaviors, demographics, challenges, and motives. In other words, what is going to make these customers want to click on your ads. As we will elaborate, the best way to go about this is to map out your ideal customer personas and adapt the ads in your campaign based on your target customers' preferences and elements of the buying process.

Customer Segmenting – Building Customer Personas

The first thing you have to do is narrow down your target audience based on their demographics and psychographics. Always remember that your customers, whether current or prospective, are your most valuable asset and will be the reason behind your success or failure. Research every single factor related to them whether it is their age ranges, education, housing/location, occupations, means of transport, family status, and leisure activities. It is important that you understand their attitude, personality, opinions, value systems, and interests.

By understanding this info, you can extract who your ideal customer personas are and customize ads tailored for them.

So what are the sources through which we can identify customer's needs?

The best way to go about this is to start off by researching your current customers. Analyze your website's Google Analytics and check the demographics of your current traffic. Crosscheck what you already know about your customers.

Speak to your current customers. Send them surveys asking about their hobbies, occupation and family status. Find out why they chose your company, what the benefits that appealed to them are.

Speak with your sales team, find out who they think the best customers are and what they already know about them and their habits.

Search social media and visit Q&A websites such as Quora and search for questions that you believe your target customers would be interested in discussing. This will help you brainstorm, as well as to understand the slang of your prospects.

Search Google to find out average annual incomes, hobbies and interests. Read Industry research reports, papers and presentations, news articles and industry expert interviews.

Sometimes, you will have to make educated judgements based on partial information available from research. Don't hesitate to do that.

You should end up with a table such as this:

Persona Fictional Name	Age	Family Status	Annual Income	Challenges	What experience they seek	Where do they go online for information

Understanding your different target personas and segments, helps in creating high quality content and messages which appeal exactly to a specific segment. When you think about it, what is the point of spending money on marketing and content if your target audience isn't interested in it? We can use a divide and rule policy – whereby we are splitting our target customers into different personas and attacking each of the personas with a tailor made advertising campaign targeting their specific needs. Using personas and dedicated campaigns for each of the personas helps keep the campaign performance high.

Let's take for example, an imaginary high-end air conditioning company that provides air conditioners that heat and cool silently within minutes.

Let's call it AirKings

AirKings provide costly air conditioners mainly to luxury apartments and houses.

Here is AirKings' target persona table:

Persona Fictional Name	Age	Family Status	Annual Income	Challenges	What experience they seek	Where do they go online for information
George, Luxury Apartment Owner	35	Recently married with no kids.	US$ 200,000	Making life as comfortable as possible Impressing peers keeping up-to-date with the best home improvement technologies	A reliable company who will be clean professional and provide premium service at non-conventional hours	Home Improvement blogs and forums. Google. Facebook.
Hillary, Luxury home Owner	47	Married with grownup kids.	US$ 500,000	Hillary conducts dinners and benefits at her house; she spends time trying to improve the place and keep it presentable. Cooling and heating a large house quietly.	Hilary does not let random people into her house. She would want recommendations and do her due diligence before enabling any constructor inside her "fortress".	Home Improvement magazines and architects and interior designer's forums.
Joe, Architect / Interior Designer	40	Married with young kids	US$ 150,000	Finding reliable vendors to work with long term and provide service for their wealthy customers	long term, mutual and beneficial cooperation	Architect and Interior Designer consumer magazines, blogs, forums, and industry publications and professional forums.

Based on these personas, AirKings will be able to tailor their advertising and marketing campaigns based on these customer types. For Search campaigns they will be able to smartly choose suitable keywords focusing on the personas challenges, and for display campaigns they will be able to tailor messages to their target personas on relevant websites.

The Customer Buying Process

Need / Problem Recognition

At this stage, the prospects will use phrases related to their problem / need with respect to their level of awareness to their need. These search phrases are called Keywords. Smart advertising will tailor different keywords in accordance with the prospects awareness level.

Continuing with AirKings, the main need / problem recognition of customers at a low awareness level would focus on:

- Making life as comfortable as possible
- Impressing peers
- High end home improvement

A high awareness level would focus on:

Quick and quiet air conditioners

Note that the further we drift from keywords that describe the problem precisely, our costs will raise. As a rule of thumb, long tail keywords are cheaper than short tail ones. Long tail keywords are keywords that are more than 2-3 words which describe the product or service being searched in more detail. These long tail keywords usually have lower traffic - lower competition and thus lower CPC. Short tail keywords or head keywords are keywords that are one or two words or phrases. Short tail keywords are more commonly searched – they have high traffic with high competition and higher CPCs.

If AirKings are marketing smartly, their target personas will encounter them by:

1. Regularly browsing websites, they normally visit, and seeing a relevant ad that AirKings published via the GDN on home improvement and lifestyle sites. Such an ad will be aimed at making their target personas realize that they have a need/problem and trigger their curiosity.

2. Moving them up to the information gathering stage where they will directly search for a solution by typing a term such as "quick and quiet air conditioners" on Google and encountering a relevant ad that AirKings published via the GSN

Be sure to understand your target customer personas and how you can help solve their needs and challenges.

Information Gathering

This stage involves the process of information gathering done by your prospective customer.

On the example of AirKings, their channels for information gathering can range from seeking advice on their personal network to searching the web for recommended solutions.

The search for information on the web may involve visiting websites they would go to for information and searching on Google.

Understanding this research / information gathering process gives you an idea on where to reach your prospects. It lets you know what your personas are looking for, their sources of information, how they acquire it, what are the trust factors, what information they consider important to make their decision. This stage provides you insights into where to reach the customer and what feature-benefits to include in your ads.

The main purpose for developing your search advertising campaign from this stage is the list of short term keywords prospects use for searching for a solution.

Example: Continuing with AirKings, George, Luxury Apartment Owner will search Google for terms regarding heating and cooling air conditioners for apartments. Various websites will provide him with information on prices, heating and cooling air conditioning products, rank air conditioning companies, who provide relevant products and services. In other words, it will provide him information he is seeking before making a purchasing decision.

A smart GSN campaign will ensure the AirKings show up in search results when George searches the above.

A complementary GDN campaign will ensure AirKings will show up when George browses relevant websites.

Alternatives Evaluation

This is the comparison phase of the buying process where the prospective customer arrives at alternatives based on the information gathered in the previous phase and compares them on various parameters to see what the best fit is for them.

Example: George is looking for quiet and fast heating and cooling air conditioners. At this stage AirKings would best follow him around the web with Google Display Remarketing ads, making sure he is frequently reminded of their existence and highlighting their expertise and how dedicated they are to each project they take on.

Purchase Decision

This stage of the buying process involves the act of acquiring the product or service itself. Once the decision is made on what to buy - how is it executed?

What are the elements that are involved in the buying process? Where do they buy the product / service from – online or brick and mortar stores? What support do they require when buying?

Continuing with the AirKings example, George saw AirKing's ads on GSN as well as GDN, and has decided to buy their air conditioners online which come with a 10-year warranty period and an economical annual maintenance with the first year free.

These insights can be used to structure the ad extensions. We will explain about extensions in later chapters.

Chapter 3: Understanding Your Unique Selling Proposition (USP)

Once you have a better idea of who you are talking to – the next step is to understand what you are offering them. Try to understand this on an overall company mission level and then zoom in to understand your current campaign offer.

Your USP summarizes what your company mission is and what distinguishes you from your competition. Why should a customer pick you over the other alternatives available in the marketplace? In a crowded marketplace with many products and services coexisting with very narrow differences – it's the USP that will set you apart to get noticed by your target customers.

Here are some examples of remarkable USPs by famous brands describing how they are different using their slogan:

Avis Car Rental – "We are number two. We try harder".

Domino's Pizza – "Fresh, Hot Pizzas delivered to your door within 30 minutes or it's free".

Fedex - "When your package absolutely, positively has to get there overnight".

M&Ms - "The milk chocolate melts in your mouth, not in your hand".

British Airways- "The World's Favorite Airline".

Apple – "Think Different".

Make a list of your entire product or service's features. Know exactly why a customer should choose your product or service.

Once you have listed the features the fun begins. See how you can turn each feature into a compelling benefit. Back to the AirKings example, one of their core features is quick air heating. This is a feature. Describing it "as is" is hardly convincing. Help your prospects understand what they are gaining out of this feature. Consider the experience they are seeking. We know AirKing's prospects are looking for an air conditioner company they can trust and can help make their lives more comfortable. How about this copy - "Airkings - when it's unbearably hot, every second your house takes to cool down counts".

Sounds more like it, right?

Do this as a rule of thumb. Take each feature and turn it into a benefit. Make sure the benefit is crystal clear. Technical descriptions are usually boring, not convincing, and will hardly help you stand out and convince your prospective customers to choose you.

An interesting way to do this is to think about this is to think what would make you want to click on an ad or read it?

Once you have an idea of who you are talking to and what your USP is, you can dive into the next step – understanding Google AdWords.

Chapter 4: Quick Overview of how AdWords Works

Google AdWords provide a wide variety of mediums to advertise on. These mediums include the Google search engines and Google partner search engines such as AOL.

Via Display advertising (which reaches 83% of the world's websites and mobile applications) you can advertise static banners as well as dynamic HTML5 banners, video ads and interstitial ads.

Bidding on those placements can be done using the following bidding methods:

- Pay Per Click (PPC) – you pay only when someone clicks your ad – popular with search advertising with a specific action driving objective like a purchase or a signup.

- Pay Per Mil (thousand) (PPM) – you pay when someone views your ad – popular with display advertising with a branding / awareness generation objective.

- Pay Per View (PPV) – this is popular in video advertising with a branding / awareness generation objective.

Choosing the bidding and advertising medium will always depend on your goals and budget.

The Basic Cycle of Working of AdWords

When you start using Google AdWords, every dollar you spend should be taken into consideration carefully. If you start investing your money in certain keywords or ads and realize they are not leading to positive results, it's an alert to reassess your strategy. The advantage in Google AdWords is you can see the number of people who saw your ad, the number of people who clicked on your ads to visit your website, and the leads generated from your ads.

In essence, AdWords is an auction system. The ads that are displayed are the ones that won the auction. Every time a search is conducted on Google, an auction takes place. Winning results are based on the Ad Ranks. Ranks are calculated by multiplying the Quality Score of the ad and the bid amount. Quality Score is a metric which assesses account relevance and landing page factors. It is an estimate of the quality of your keywords, ads and landing pages on a scale of 1-10 and is determined every time a customer searches a keyword you are targeting.

Quality Score X bid amount = Ad Rank

The more relevant your ads and landing pages are, the higher your quality score – resulting in a higher ad rank, higher ad position and lower cost per click.

The three components of Quality Score are:

1. Expected Click Through Rate

2. Ad Relevance

3. Landing Page Experience.

We will elaborate on this later on but first let's start by understanding the different campaign types we can use.

Types of Campaigns

1. Search Campaigns

2. Display Campaigns

3. Search with Display Select

4. Remarketing Campaigns (Display and Search)

5. Video Ad campaigns

6. Google Shopping Campaigns

7. Universal App Campaigns

Search Campaigns

You can setup a campaign targeting the Google Search Network (GSN) consists of Google Search, Google Maps, Google Shopping, and many Non-Google Search Partner websites like AOL that show Google Ads matched to search queries. On the GSN you can setup campaigns to show your ads along with SERPS.

The Ad format available for Search Campaigns is Text Ads.

On GSN you can target campaigns to specific locations, time, and devices. These campaigns are keyword based. We will elaborate on that but for now what you should know is that on GSN when people search the keywords you are targeting, if your bid wins, your ads will be displayed to them along with the search results on Google Search. If anyone clicks your ad, you will pay for the click. AKA Pay Per Click (PPC).

Here is an example of different GSN winning bids for the keywords "Mens Shoes"

Display Campaigns

You can setup a Display campaign targeting The Google Display Network (GDN) which aggregates about 83% of the world's advertising inventory or advertising space on websites across the world including Google Websites like Google Finance, Google Blogger, YouTube, and Gmail, a host of Google Partner sites, Mobiles sites and Mobile Apps.

Ad formats available for Display Campaigns are Text Ads, Image Ads, Rich Media Ads and Video Ads.

Here is an example of different GDN ads:

Search with Display Select

If you want to try out AdWords with the least amount of effort – Search with Display Select is a good place to start. This campaign type enables you to use a combination of Search and Display ads targeting both the search and display campaign from one single campaign. This is recommended only for beginners, as search only and display only campaigns have better targeting features that help them perform better.

Ad formats available for Search with Display Select campaigns are Text Ads, Image Ads, Rich Media Ads and Video Ads.

Remarketing Campaigns (Display and Search)

Remarketing campaigns target prospective customers who visited your website previously while they browse the internet. These prospective customers are people who have visited your website but not taken a specific action you wanted them to – like make a purchase, fill a form, download a whitepaper or e-book, click to call you, etc. Remarketing campaigns have to be setup separately for search and display networks. Remarketing for Search is also known as Remarketing Lists for Search Ads (RLSA). We will talk about Remarketing campaigns in detail in a separate chapter on how to set up and optimize them.

Ad formats available for Display Remarketing Campaigns are Text Ads, Image Ads, Rich Media Ads.

For Search Remarketing Campaigns only Text Ad format is available.

Video Ad Campaigns

You can create video ad campaigns which run on YouTube and other Google Partner websites. Video Ads have shot up in importance as YouTube is the second largest search engine in the world after Google Search. You can target YouTube with other ad formats like text ads and display ads from the display campaigns.

Ad formats available for Video Campaigns are display video ads and in steaming video ads.

Google Shopping Campaigns

If you are selling a product, you can setup your product ads through Google Shopping Campaigns targeting people who are searching for the product you offer. Google Shopping Campaigns displays your product images, price and your business name. Google Shopping Campaigns let you show your product specific ads across devices when people are searching products that you offer. Google Shopping Campaigns provides features which allow you to showcase your local inventory from the closest store (in case you are a multi store retailer), and stand out as a trusted store, with promotional offers, and product ratings.

Universal App Campaigns

Universal App Campaigns target specific goals like mobile app installation and engagement across GSN, GDN, Mobile app network AdMob and YouTube. This campaign type is automated and requires very little effort to set up making it very easy for driving mobile app installs. Universal App Campaigns can be setup from the Google Play Developer Console or AdWords. You can provide up to four lines of ad text which can be used interchangeably including an option to run video ads through YouTube. The targeting options are limited to location and language.

This campaign type works on a Cost Per Install (CPI) bid strategy. Once you setup the campaign, the ads are generated and the campaign is optimized automatically to deliver mobile app installs based on the CPI targets.

Chapter 5: Setting up a Search Ad Campaign

To setup a Search campaign go to the AdWords console and click on the "+ Campaign" Red Button and select "Search Network Only" as indicated in the illustration below.

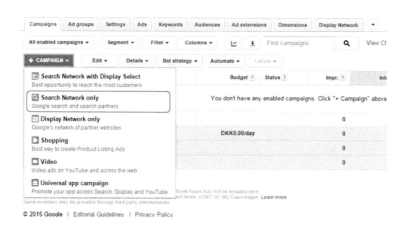

After selecting "Search Network Only", the next screen will ask you to select specific objectives for the campaign like Mobile App Installs, Mobile App Engagement, Dynamic Search Ads and Call Only Ads. Apart from these, there are a couple of options in the Campaign Sub-Type – "Standard" and "All features". 'Standard Features' lets you use targeting of basic location, language, bidding, budget settings and some ad extensions. Standard Features is a simplified version of search campaigns which enables you to get out of the blocks faster.

We recommend using the 'All Features' option which includes all Standard Features along with Mobile Settings, Ad Delivery Method, all Ad Extensions and also target Google Search Partner websites. This gives you a better control on your campaign.

5.1 Keywords Targeting

Search Campaigns use keywords or phrases that are relevant to your product or service, to show ads to potential customers searching for similar terms on Google or its search partners' websites. Targeting will vary based on the keyword match type.

These campaigns will show up when a search is initiated. It's very important to map out what your different personas would be looking for and to then make sure your ads will show up once prospects are searching for your brand or solution.

Keyword Classification

Keywords can be classified into top of the funnel, middle of the funnel and bottom of the funnel. This classification is necessary because not all keywords or phrases are equal.

At the bottom of the funnel are keywords which are closest to conversions e.g.: direct brand searches such as "Buy AirKing Air Conditioner" or direct need searches such as "Buy Air Conditioner" or "Buy Quiet Air Conditioner" where the intent of the search is very clear – the customer has already decided what solution they need and is ready to act.

The middle of the funnel keywords shows an intent whereby the prospective customer is looking to compare and view reviews of products or services e.g. "Review of Air Conditioner Companies or "Reviews of Best Quiet Air Conditioners" – these customers need to be nurtured before they are ready to buy.

The top of the funnel keywords is those that are keywords or phrases used for initial research about a product or services and are the farthest away from buying or converting e.g.: "Air Conditioners" or even further, phrases used for broader research at an unaware stage such as – "home improvement". Note however that we do not recommend using GSN for unaware stages. We recommend focusing on the GDN for very broad top of the funnel keywords such as home improvement as the chances of generating ROI for such terms on GSN are scarce. This classification of keywords helps you to decide on the bids as well as the content of the landing pages to take the customer close to buying.

The cost per click, competition and conversions are all different for keywords depending on which phase of the funnel they are in. If it's the bottom of the funnel keywords – they usually have higher cost per click, the competition is higher and the conversions are also higher. Whereas if it's the top of the funnel keywords the cost per clicks are lower, the competition is lower and the conversions rate is also very low.

Therefore, it is very critical to classify your keywords and write ads differently for each of them and to have separate landing pages for each stage.

Campaign Structuring and Keyword Categorization

Your AdWords account consists of campaigns and ad groups. Each campaign has its own budget, settings and where the ads are shown. While ad groups are a set of tightly themed keywords which you want to show your ads in. For example, AirKings can structure their campaign based on search terms used by a customer to look for air conditioners like Best Air Conditioners, Quick Cooling Air Conditioners, Quiet Air Conditioners, Air Conditioning Companies, etc and then create ad groups of tightly themed specific search terms like in the Best Air Conditioners Ad Group – will have these keywords – Best Air Conditioners, Best Air Conditioning, top 10 best air conditioners, air conditioners best, etc.

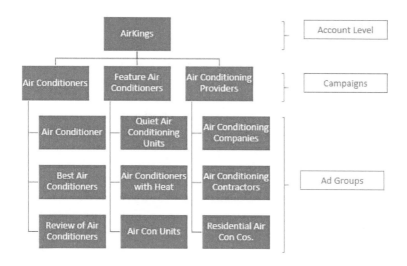

Keyword List Development / Keyword Research

First, list down all the possible terms a customer associates with your product or service. Second, align your keywords with marketing objectives. Go for broader keywords to target a larger audience and more specific keywords when you want to target a precise customer segment. Thirdly, you need to group keywords that are closely themed or similar in nature into ad groups. Keep in mind that whatever you choose - broad or specific, your keywords should be relevant to your ads, website and those keywords or their synonyms should also be present on your website ideally. Keywords of two or more words (phrases) tend to work effectively.

You can use the Keyword Planning Tool on AdWords to get keyword ideas and other keyword data like search volume, bid suggestions, competition for keywords, keyword grouping ideas, etc. The Keyword Planning Tool also helps you to see how a list of keywords may perform and choose competitive bids and budgets.

Now let's look at how to develop a keyword list. Put yourself in the customer's shoes and list out the various keywords and terms that they use to identify and describe your business / service. Continuing with the AirKings example – AirKings can describe its offering as "Air Conditioners", "Quiet Air Conditioners", "Efficient Air Conditioners", "Quick Air Conditioners", "Heating and Cooling Air Conditioners", "Home Air Conditioner Units", "Residential Air Conditioners", etc. AirKings can expand this keyword list by adding destination names to the keywords – like if they are looking for USA, New York, etc. related keywords – the keywords / phrases will be "Residential Air Conditioners in USA". "Home Air Conditioning Contractors in New York", etc. and they can add product names and specifications as well like "3-ton residential air conditioners" "central air conditioners", etc.

It's recommended that you select specific keywords that are close to your business to start off – as specific keywords very closely related to your business will generate relatively less traffic than broad keywords and therefore the campaign will quickly move to generate conversions. For example, AirKings should choose specific keywords like "Air Conditioning Companies" and "Quiet Air Conditioners" – which closely describe what they are offering – rather than choose broad terms like "air conditioners", "air con units", etc. Note that the more specific the search terms the lower the traffic volume there will be – so if you only choose search terms that are too specific to your business you will find it difficult to reach many people. Once the campaign has been successful with a set of keywords that are closely related to your business / product / service – then we can expand the keywords to include broader keywords to increase coverage to a larger audience.

Keywords need to be grouped into tightly themed ad groups based on your products / services. This will enable you to keep your AdWords account better organized and relevant for customers who are searching for your products. Example – all "quiet air conditioner" related keywords needs to be clubbed into an ad group. Ideally the number of keywords per ad group should be between 5 and 20 and keywords that have 2 or 3 words perform better than one word keywords or keywords / phrases that are 4 words or more.

Keyword Planning Tool

You can use the Keyword Planning Tool in AdWords to research your keywords. The Keyword Tool can be accessed by clicking on the Tools Link in the header of the AdWords Console. The Keyword Tool provides you related keywords, ad grouping ideas and traffic estimates including historical statistics and traffic forecasts, thus helping you in deciding the keywords list that you need to be targeted in your campaign.

Illustration: Keyword Planner Tool in AdWords

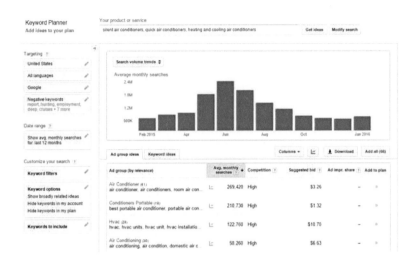

The Keyword Planner can be used to generate a list of keywords for a new campaign or expand the keyword list for an existing campaign. The keyword list can be generated based on an initial list of keywords (also known as seed keywords) or a website or a category. As the keyword planner lists a lot of related keywords you can specifically select individual keyword or ad groups based on how closely related they are to the product / service you are advertising for.

The Keyword Planner also helps you forecast the clicks you can get from a given budget by means of reviewing the shortlisted keywords and giving a max bid and budget for the campaign. So you can technically give different bids to see how many clicks you get. The

Keyword Planner forecasting also allows you to estimate the budget required for the campaign.

Keywords Match Types

'Broad match' type targets a wider audience, while on the other end 'exact match' targets a very specific audience.

Broad Match

'Broad Match' keyword type is a default keyword match type in AdWords. With 'Broad match type' your ads will be shown to search terms which contain your keywords in any order or with any other keywords. Your Ads will also be displayed for any closely related or close variations of the keywords being targeted. The ads are shown for searches including misspellings, synonyms, related searches and other relevant variations.

Example: If your keyword is Air Conditioner, your ad will get triggered when people search for air conditioners, but it also triggers the ad for unrelated searches like hair conditioners.

Broad Modified Match (BMM)

'Broad Modified Match' keyword type uses a modifier '+' – a plus sign to any search term that is part of the broad match keyword phrase. By adding this plus sign in front of any word within a term, you can control the ads to be shown on terms which include the words marked with the plus sign. The ads are shown for searches which contain the terms within any variation, but not synonyms or related search terms.

Example: If your keyword is "+Best +Air +Conditioners", your ad will be displayed when people search for any variation using the all three keywords. For example, when people search for "**best** companies for **air conditioners**" (using only some of the words for example "companies for **air conditioners**" will not trigger the ad).

Phrase Match

Phrase Match Keyword Type enables ads to be shown to searches which are exactly the same as the keyword and also those that include terms before and after the targeted keyword. Phrase match enables you to target specific search terms along with closely related ones and reduces your ads being shown for unrelated search terms. A phrase match keyword is used with quotation marks before and after the keyword like "keyword". Close variations of the keyword will also trigger the ads.

Example: If your keyword is "air conditioner", your ad will be displayed for search terms like "air conditioners", but will not trigger ads for searches like "best air conditioners".

Exact Match

Exact match keyword type triggers an ad only when the search term is exactly the keyword you are targeting without any other term with your keyword. When the search terms are close variations of the keyword you are targeting, then the ads are triggered as well. Ads won't trigger when there are additional words in the search term unlike phrase match. To use exact match keyword type, add "[ ]" brackets around the keyword like [keyword].

Example: If your keyword is air conditioners, your ads will be displayed for the search terms [air conditioners] and not for [best air conditioners].

Negative Match

Negative Match type can be used to not show your ads when certain terms appear in a search. Negative match is used to be more specific with keyword targeting and remove all irrelevant traffic. For using the negative match just add a "−" sign before the keyword.

Example: If your keyword is "air conditioners", you can use negative match for the term "cheap" by adding "−cheap". So your ads will not trigger for keywords that contain the term "cheap" like "cheap air conditioners". This way you will restrict people who are looking for a budget or cheap deals on air conditioners.

Negative match type can be used with other match keyword types as well. For example, you don't want to trigger your ads for specific exact search terms – you can add them as negatives this way "– [cheap]".

Example: If your negative match keyword is – [commercial], your ads will not trigger for search terms [commercial air conditioners] and ads will trigger for search terms [residential air conditioners].

Illustration: Quick Recap of the Match Types

Match Type	Symbol	Ads show for searches	Example Keyword	Example Search Terms for which Ads will show
Broad	None	including misspellings, synonyms, related searches, and other relevant variations	air conditioner	best air conditioners, air conditioners for homes, etc.
Modified Broad	+keyword	contain the modified term (or close variations, but not synonyms), in any order	+air +conditioners	best air conditioners, residential air conditioners
Phrase	"keyword"	are a phrase, and close variations of that phrase	"air conditioner"	"best air conditioners", "residential air conditioners"
Exact	[keyword]	are an exact term and close variations of that exact term	[home air conditioner]	[home air conditioner]
Negative	-keyword	are searches without the term	-cheap	air conditioners – will trigger the add, while [cheap air conditioner] will not trigger the ad

Illustration: Keyword Match Types as they Appear on the AdWords Console

		Keyword	Status ?	Max. CPC ?	Match ↑ type ?	Clicks ?	Impr. ?	CTR ?	Avg. CPC ?	Cost ?	Avg. Pos. ?
☐	●	[air conditioner]	Eligible	$10.00	Exact	0	0	0.00%	$0.00	$0.00	0.0
☐	●	air conditioner	Eligible	$10.00	Broad	0	0	0.00%	$0.00	$0.00	0.0
☐	●	+air +conditioner	Eligible	$10.00	Broad	0	0	0.00%	$0.00	$0.00	0.0
☐	●	"air conditioner"	Eligible	$10.00	Phrase	0	0	0.00%	$0.00	$0.00	0.0
		Total - all enabled keywords ?		--		0	0	0.00%	$0.00	$0.00	0.0
		Total - all experiments ?		--		0	0	0.00%	$0.00	$0.00	0.0
		Total - all ad group ?		--		0	0	0.00%	$0.00	$0.00	0.0

Bonus Tip: Conduct Competitor Keyword Research

What keywords are your competitors using?

There are various tools that can be used for conducting competitive research from simple website visits, Google searches to tools like SpyFu, SEM Rush, iSpionage and many others.

The trick is not to believe all the data fully from the tools - as these tools pickup data from various sources and not directly from your competitor's AdWords account. We recommend collating all the information from the tools and average-out the findings and use it more as a directional resource.

5.2 Location, Language and Device Targeting

Location Targeting helps focus your ads where potential customers are located. Location Targeting allows you to target the entire country (e.g. USA), or specific regions, states or cities (e.g. Chicago City or New Jersey State) or certain distances around your business (e.g. 10 Miles around New Brunswick in New Jersey State).

The same way you include location targets, you can also exclude location from targeting. For Example, AirKings wants to run ads for people across USA, but exclude Alaska – they will be able to do it by adding Alaska as an exclusion location target.

Illustration: Location Targeting in AdWords

There are advanced location targeting options available which will help you fine-tune your location targeting further by including or excluding these options. The 'Include' options are: People in, searching for and interested in your target location; people in my target location; and people searching for and interested in your target location. Google targets people based on their physical location as well as people who are searching for or show interest in a target location.

Example – If AirKings is targeting customers from Chicago and has set their location target for Chicago City and neighborhoods for Home Air Conditioners.

If the first advanced location targeting option of "People in, searching for and interested in your target location" is chosen, AirKings ads will show to a person who is physically located in New York City if he is searching for "Air Conditioner companies in Chicago".

If the second advanced location targeting option of "people in my target location" is chosen, AirKings ads will not show for a person who is physically located in New York City if he is searching for "Air Conditioners".

If the third advanced location targeting option of "people searching for and interested in your target location" is chosen, AirKings ads will show to a person who is physically located in New York City if he is searching for "Air Conditioners in Chicago".

Similarly, the exclusion of advanced location targeting also works. You can exclude people in the target locations you have excluded or you can exclude people in, searching for or who are interested in your excluded locations.

Illustration: Advanced Location Options in AdWords

⊟ Location options (advanced)

Target ? • People in, searching for, or who show interest in my targeted location (recommended) ?
○ People in my targeted location ?
○ People searching for, or who show interest in my targeted location ?

Exclude ? • People in, searching for, or who show interest in my excluded location (recommended) ?
○ People in my excluded location ?

Language targeting helps you to focus your ads to customers who speak a particular language. Note that AdWords doesn't translate ads, so you will have to create ads in the language you are targeting.

Illustration: Language Targeting in AdWords

Device targeting lets you target customers specifically on desktops, tablets and mobiles. For example, if your customers are on-the-go, targeting mobile devices will make sense. Most mobile devices today have full browsers and apps enabling you to target customers with different mobile ad types. Desktops and Tablets are clubbed together and ads created are by default targeted at Desktops and Tablets.

Illustration: Device Targeting in AdWords

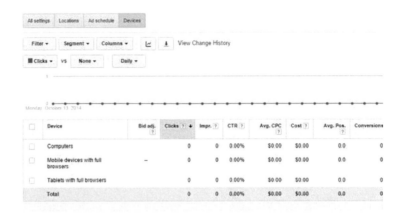

5.3 Budget and Bidding

You set a daily budget for each campaign indicating the amount you are willing to spend on an average per day for a particular campaign based on the marketing goals. You can get the daily budget by dividing the monthly budget by 30.4 (average number of days per month). It is ideal to start small and scale up based on performance.

Illustration: Setting Daily Budget in AdWords

The budget you set can also be controlled further through an advanced setting of how the budget has to be used – Standard and Accelerated. The Standard setting allows budgets to be spent evenly throughout the day and ensure that your ads are shown round the clock. While on the other hand, Accelerated setting allows you to target all the search volume, maybe using up the budget before the end of the day – thus if you choose this option be sure that you have set a substantial daily budget and so that your ad shows throughout the day.

Illustration: Budget Delivery Method in AdWords

There are a few Bidding strategies you can choose from based on your campaign's marketing objective / goal.

You can also use advanced strategies like bid adjustments to bid more or less competitively across locations, time of day and devices. In general:

The higher the bid → higher ad position→ higher number of clicks and traffic to your website.

Illustration: Bidding in AdWords

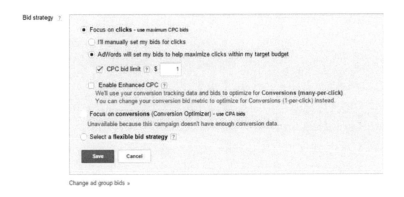

Change ad group bids »

Illustration: Marketing Objective and Bidding Strategy in AdWords

Marketing Objective	Bidding Strategy
Drive Potential Customers to your website.	Cost-Per-Click (CPC) Bidding
Brand Building and Awareness	Cost-Per-Impression (CPM) Bidding
Maximise Conversions on your website	Cost-Per-Acquisition (CPA) Bidding

Now let's look at the various bidding options in detail. Basically, there are three broad bidding options available in Search Campaigns:

1. Focus on clicks

2. Focus on conversions

3. Flexible bidding strategies.

Focus on Clicks

The Focus on Clicks (Cost Per Click or CPC) option to drive traffic to your website provides two bidding strategies:

1. Manual Cost Per Click Bidding - a default option in AdWords that enables you the flexibility to bid differently for each of your ad groups and keywords individually.

2. Automatic Cost Per Click Bidding - the simplest bidding option whereby Google AdWords automatically manages bids to maximize the number of clicks you can generate with the given daily budget.

Focus on Conversations

Focus on Conversions (Cost Per Acquisition or CPA) is an advanced option that enables you to bid an amount that you are willing to pay per conversion or acquiring a new customer.

There are a few AdWords requirements to enable CPA based bidding like conversion tracking should be implemented and the campaign must have received at least 15 conversions in the last 30 days.

Flexible Bidding Strategies

Flexible bid strategy enables you to utilize automated bidding across campaigns with specific goals in mind. There are 6 flexible bid strategies available on AdWords and they are:

1. Maximize Clicks

2. Target Search Page Location

3. Target Outrank Share

4. Target Cost Per Acquisition (CPA)

5. Enhanced Cost Per Click (ECPC)

6. Return on Ad Spend (ROAS)

Maximize Clicks Flexible Bidding Strategy

This strategy enables you to get maximum clicks for a particular budget set. This is a flexible version of the automatic bidding option. This strategy can be used to increase clicks from low traffic keywords in ad groups and campaigns.

Target Search Page Location Bidding Strategy

This strategy enables you to target the first page or the top of the first page by automatically adjusting bids. This strategy can be used to get high visibility for your ads.

Target Outrank Share Bidding Strategy

This strategy enables you to outrank a particular domain which is also advertising on a specific set of keywords through automatic bid adjustments. This strategy can be employed for getting more visibility for your ads than a particular competitor domain.

Target Cost Per Acquisition Bidding Strategy

This strategy enables you to get maximum conversions around a particular Cost Per Acquisition set in the campaign by automatically adjusting bids. This strategy can be employed to get more conversions at a target Cost Per Acquisition.

Enhanced Cost Per Click Bidding Strategy

This strategy enables you to automatically increase or decrease your bids based on the likelihood of conversions. This strategy can be employed to get more conversions while being in control of keywords bids.

Return on Ad Spend Bidding Strategy

This strategy enables you to maximize the conversion value by automatically adjusting bids to reach a target return on ad spend. This strategy can be employed when you generate a target conversion value on ad spend.

5.4 Ad Scheduling

The campaigns can have a start and end date – this enables you to run campaigns for a specific time period.

The ads can also be scheduled to run during specific times of the day as well. This enables you to do advertising only when there is a need or during specific parts of the day. For example, a restaurant wants to advertise its all new authentic Italian lunch menu to its target audience within a 3-mile radius of its restaurant. There is no point in advertising throughout the day – so the restaurant can set specific lunch hours to run its ads to draw traffic during lunch.

Illustration: Ad Scheduling in AdWords

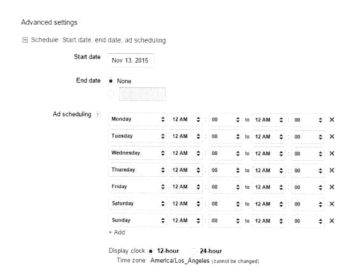

5.5 Ad Rotation Settings

This setting is used to define how different ads in your ads groups should be rotated and on what basis. The options available are:

1. Optimize for Clicks

2. Optimize for Conversions

3. Rotate evenly

4. Rotate indefinitely

Optimize for Clicks

This option enables ads to be shown which are providing the highest clicks and which have the highest click through rate (clicks divided by impressions – we will explain this in detail later).

Optimize for Conversions

This option enables you to show ads that are converting the most. This is a recommended option to be used for generating higher conversions by using the automatic conversion optimization of AdWords based on conversions.

Important Note - this option has to be used when no other optimization solution or AB testing is being conducted, as those will provide wrong signals to AdWords and automatic optimization may not yield results in the long run.

Rotate Evenly

This option ensures that your ads get an equal share of impressions for a period of 90 days and that post 90 days they will be optimized for conversions. Using this ensures that there is statistical significance for AdWords to automatically start optimizing for conversions. This option can be used when there are other conversion optimization tools or methods executed simultaneously such as A/B testing for a landing page.

Rotate Indefinitely

This option shows all ads equally and doesn't optimize at all. We don't recommend ever using this option.

Illustration: Ad Rotation in AdWords

Once we have input the campaign settings – click on the **Save and Continue** button.

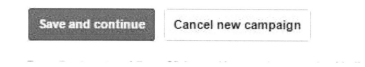

5.6 Creating Ad Groups

Now that you've selected and created your campaign and completed your settings, we can start creating our first ad group. To create an ad group – click on the red **"+ AD GROUP"** button.

The next step is to give the ad group a name and proceed to create your first ad copy.

Illustration: Creating Search Ads and Ad Groups in AdWords

First let's get to know the basics of a Search ad. A typical text ad consists of a headline, two description lines and a display URL (web address). There are restrictions to the number of characters in the headline and description lines.

Headline: 25 characters

Description Line 1: 35 characters

Description Line 2: 35 characters

Display URL: 35 characters

We will go into details of how to write ad copy and Copy Testing of Ads later in the chapter.

Types of Ads

There are several ad types that can be created on Google AdWords depending on the type and objective of the campaign. The different ad types are: text ads, image ads, video ads, and rich media ads (flash ads). Each of the ads types are self-explanatory.

Ad Type	Used in Campaign Type	Benefits
Text Ads	Search	Reaches Customers who are looking for your product
Image Ads	Display	Visually showcases your product / service to customers who are browsing online
App Ads	Search, Display	Reach your Customers on-the-go
Video Ads	Display	Reach your Customers while they are browsing online with a rich experience
Rich Media Ads	Display	Reach your Customers while they are browsing online with a rich experience
Product Listing Ads	Search	Reach your Customers while they are searching for your products/services with a visual
Call Only Ads	Mobile Search	Reach your Customers on-the-go to drive phone calls

All Ads are reviewed by Google to see if they meet all Google policies and only approved ads are eligible to be shown to the customers. The time taken for ad approval can vary from a few minutes to a few hours

5.7 Ad Copy Writing

Now is the time to combine what you have already defined regarding your company USP and target customer personas, with your current campaign offering.

Here are key points to consider:

- What makes this offer different from that of your competitors

- What action do you want your prospect to take?

- What do you want your target personas to feel about our offering?

- What is the deadline for the offer / promotion / exclusive?

- How does this offer solve your target personas needs/ wants/ pain points?

Technical Rules of Thumb:

1. Include at least one keyword in your ad to make it relevant for potential customers to click your ads.

2. Match the content of your designated landing page to the ad text in order to ensure there is a message match.

3. Include a killer CTA (call to action) - tell potential customers how they can buy from you or contact you. Use words like Get a Free Quote, Call Today, etc.

Make sure to experiment with your ad copy. Try different ad texts, use different messages and create 3-4 ads per ad group.

5.8 Types of Ad Extensions

Ad extensions provide additional information about your business within your ads. This normally results in higher clicks / traffic to your website.

The various Ad extensions are Call Extensions, Site-link Extensions, Location Extensions, App Extensions, Review Extensions and Callout Extensions. All of the above are manual extensions, while there are some automated extensions as well like ratings and social (Google+) extensions.

Illustration: Description of Ad Extensions in AdWords

Extensions	What is it?
Call Extensions	Display of phone number and click-to-call feature
Site-link Extensions	Links to other related sections / pages of your website
Location Extensions	Helps customers to find your business - Map Pin and navigation assistance
App Extensions	Link to Download App
Review Extensions	Showcase positive 3rd party reviews from well-known sources
Callout Extensions	Description of what you have to offer
Ratings	Displays Consumer and Seller ratings
Social (G+) extensions	Displays number of Google+ followers your business has

Illustration: Ad Extensions Selection in AdWords

Ad extensions

You can use this optional feature to include relevant business information with your ads. Take a tour

Location [?] ☐ Extend my ads with location information
Sitelinks [?] ☐ Extend my ads with links to sections of my site
Call [?] ☐ Extend my ads with a phone number
App [?] ☐ Extend my ads with a link to a mobile/tablet app.
Reviews [?] ☐ Extend my ads with reviews
Callouts [?] ☐ Extend my ads with additional descriptive text

5.9 Conversion Tracking

By installing a conversion tracking code on your website, you can easily track the conversions / goals that have come through your AdWords campaigns. Conversions can be any of these desired actions taken by the potential customer after clicking through from your ad - purchase of your products / services, fill out a call back form, downloaded your eBook or signed-up for newsletter.

Conversion tracking is very granular and lets you know which campaign, ad, and keyword has caused the conversion. Armed with this information you can optimize your AdWords campaign by retaining the ones that provide the best results and removes the ones that performed poorly or wasted money.

To enable the conversion tracking – go to the Tools section on top and click on the Conversions section.

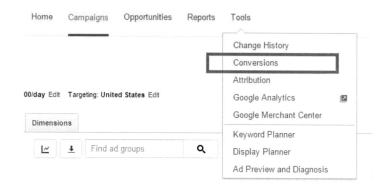

Once on the conversions page click on the **+Conversions** button.

You will have to select the Conversion you want to track - a website conversion like purchase, form submission. You can setup conversion tracking for Mobile App Downloads, Phone Calls and also import conversion tracking data from other conversions tracking systems.

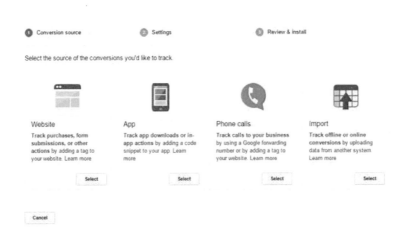

Once you select the conversion you want to track, name and save it.

After you save it – you will be provided with an html code that has to be inserted into the html code on the Thank You page, the page that is displayed after the visitor has completed the Conversion event like Purchase or Form Submission.

Once this code is inserted into the Thank You page – you can then start tracking conversions that are generated through AdWords.

Now the campaign will be ready to go live. Congratulations - You have created your first Search Campaign!

Chapter 6: Setting Up a Display Campaign

Display Advertising

This chapter highlights how to setup a display advertising campaign.

Google Display Network (GDN)

Google Display Network or GDN consists of over 2 million websites including Google properties like Google Finance, Gmail, Blogger, YouTube and a host of other websites and mobile apps that have partnered with Google to show Google ads. GDN reaches 83% of Internet users worldwide.

GDN enables advertisers to target ads to customers who are surfing the internet with an ability to target specific interests and choose where the ads should appear (websites and web pages) with a variety of ad formats including Text ads, Image Ads, Video Ads and Rich Media Ads.

With GDN you can achieve a wide range of marketing objectives:

a. Building brand awareness (For Example, AirKings will be targeting Home Improvement, Interior Design and Home Décor to generate awareness among the target audience about their brand and products.)

b. Influence your target personas during their consideration stage.

c. Driving specific actions:

- buy on your website

- fill out a form

- call your business

- visit your business

- specific goals of installing and engaging with mobile apps.

To get started with a display campaign, click on the **+ Campaign** red button and select **Display Network only**.

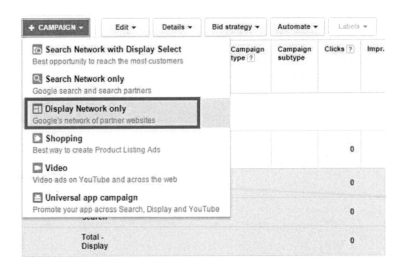

The next step is to choose the marketing objective you want to achieve through the display campaign.

Type: **Display Network only**

Campaign name [|]

Type ? ▦ Display Network only ▼ ● **Marketing objectives** - Just the features and options relevant to what you want to accomplish ?
                                   ○ **No marketing objective** - All available features and options

Marketing objective *New!*

Save time and create better campaigns by choosing a marketing objective. Learn more   Help me choose 💬

◉ Build awareness   ◆ Influence consideration   ⊟ Drive action

GET CUSTOMERS TO   GET CUSTOMERS TO   GET CUSTOMERS TO

☐ See your ad   ☐ Engage with your content   ☐ Buy on your website (includes
                                                                 remarketing)
                                    ☑
                           ☐ Visit your website   ☐ Take an action on your website
                                                                 (for example, fill out a form)

                                                              ☐ Call your business

                                                              ☐ Visit your business

                                                                      or

                                                              ☐ Install your mobile app

                                                                      or

                                                              ☐ Engage with your mobile app

Next select the details of the campaign setup — like
location, languages, bid, budget and ad extensions.

Locations ? Which locations do you want to target (or exclude) in your campaign?
           ○ All countries and territories
           ○ United States and Canada
           ● United States
           ○ Let me choose...

           [Enter a location to target or exclude]   Advanced search

           For example, a country, city, region, or postal code

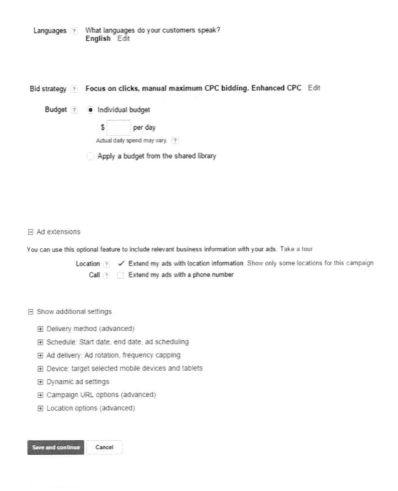

Languages [?] What languages do your customers speak?
English Edit

Bid strategy [?] **Focus on clicks, manual maximum CPC bidding. Enhanced CPC** Edit

Budget [?] ● Individual budget

$ [   ] per day
Actual daily spend may vary. [?]

○ Apply a budget from the shared library

⊟ Ad extensions

You can use this optional feature to include relevant business information with your ads. Take a tour

Location [?] ✓ Extend my ads with location information Show only some locations for this campaign
Call [?] ☐ Extend my ads with a phone number

⊟ Show additional settings

⊞ Delivery method (advanced)
⊞ Schedule: Start date, end date, ad scheduling
⊞ Ad delivery: Ad rotation, frequency capping
⊞ Device: target selected mobile devices and tablets
⊞ Dynamic ad settings
⊞ Campaign URL options (advanced)
⊞ Location options (advanced)

[Save and continue] Cancel

A status bar on top indicates in which stage you are in the display campaign creation process.

You can create ad groups with specific targeting options.

⊘ Select campaign settings   ② Create an ad group   ③ Create ads   ④ Confirmation

74

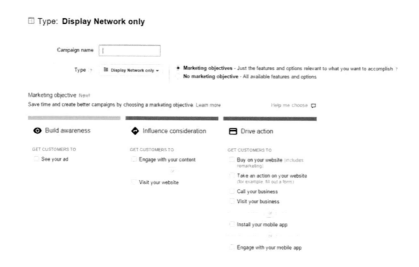

6.1 Google Display Network (GDN) Targeting

GDN enables 4 targeting options:

1. Contextual

2. Audience

3. Managed Placements Targeting

4. Demographics

Contextual Targeting

Contextual Targeting allows you to target ads to your target personas when they are browsing online using keywords or topics.

Keywords

Your display ads are eligible to show on websites whose theme or content match your keywords. Note that on GDN keywords are treated as broad match only.

1. Input your main keywords.

2. Click the "**Find related keywords**" button.

3. Google will display all relevant keywords.

4. Select the keywords you want to target. On the right hand column, you will be able to see the likely impressions you will get for the keywords selected.

Topics

Like Keywords, you can choose specific topics of interest. Your ads will be placed on websites which cater in accordance to those topics. Instead of adding words and phrases, you choose topics like "interior decoration", etc.

You can also add multiple targeting means like both keywords and topics – this way the ads will be shown only when both the criteria are met.

Audience Targeting

Interest and Remarketing

You can target your ads based on Affinity audiences, In-Market audiences and remarketing:

Affinity Audiences: You can show your ads to unique audiences based on their lifestyle, buying habits and long-term interests.

In-Market Audiences: You can show your ads to unique audiences based on their short-term lifestyle, buying habits and interests.

Remarketing: Remarketing is also known as Re-Targeting. You can reach past visitors of your websites, YouTube videos viewers and mobile apps installers through remarketing. In other words, you can show your ads to prospects who visited your website but did not perform your desired action like fill a form or make a call or purchase. Remarketing helps you to reconnect with these prospects by showing relevant ads when they browse the internet.

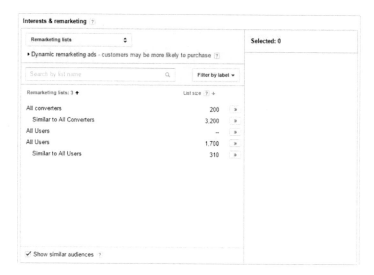

There are different types of remarketing ads:

Standard Ads show the generic ads of the brand's products or services

Dynamic remarketing ads go a step further and show ads that contain the specific products or services that the prospect browsed on your website, e.g. If a prospect browsed New York last minute flights pages on your website – dynamic ads will show New York flight ads to that prospect while he/she browses the internet.

Frequency is a game changer. Prospects who are frequently exposed to your marketing message are more likely to buy from you than someone who is hearing your marketing message for the first time.

Remarketing lists can be created based on marketing goals and specific actions the customer takes on your website. The broadest one is the "all visitors list", you can narrow it down to number of pages viewed on the website, time spent, specific pages visited, shopping cart abandoners, etc. This enables you to customize your remarketing campaigns to specific target audiences based on marketing goals.

Remarketing can be setup on your website using AdWords codes as well as Analytics codes. It is better to use analytics codes which can be later used for remarketing or retargeting campaigns on not just Google AdWords, but also other platforms like Facebook and you can target customers outside Google networks.

To create remarketing lists – Click on the Shared Library link in the left hand panel on the AdWords console.

Audiences

Remarketing reconnects you with people who are interested in your brand or business.

Create a remarketing list

Website visitors
Visitors to your website
Set up remarketing | Learn more

Mobile app users
Users of your mobile app
Create list | Learn more

YouTube users
People who interact with your YouTube channel or videos
Create list | Learn more

Customer emails
People who gave you their email addresses
Create list | Learn more

Under **Website visitors** – click on **Setup Remarketing**. You will be taken to a page that will provide you an html code to be inserted into the code of all the pages on your website. Once this code is added to all pages – AdWords will start tracking and building the remarketing lists for website visitors.

Advertisers can also remarket to those audiences that viewed your YouTube video on your YouTube channel on AdWords. Video Remarketing will help reinforce your marketing messages to an audience who are already exposed to the brand by way of viewing your videos.

YouTube remarketing lists can be created by linking YouTube and AdWords accounts, and creating a specific YouTube Remarketing list in AdWords Audiences. The same way you created the website

visitor remarketing lists you can also create a
YouTube remarketing list – just click on the "+
Remarketing List" red button in the remarketing
lists section under audiences and click on the
YouTube users button.

Name the remarketing list, specify details about the
list and then click on the "Create List" button.

To link the AdWords account to your YouTube
account – click on the gear icon on the right hand
top corner of the AdWords console and select
"Linked Accounts" – select YouTube and paste your
YouTube Channel url in the space provided and click
the Next button. You will be given an option to sign-
in to YouTube and confirm the account linking.

Managed Placements Targeting

Managed Placement Targeting allows you to place your
ads on specific websites and mobile apps you choose
from the available options. In the case of AirKings –
customers spend a lot of time on Home Improvement,
Interior Design and Interior Decoration related

websites, you can add some well-known and good content websites in these categories as Managed Placements.

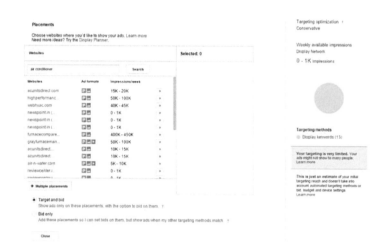

Demographics

You can choose the Demographics of your target customers. You can specifically target – Gender, Age and Parental Status.

6.2 Display Planner

Display planner can be used to create targeting for a Display Campaign. This makes it easy especially for campaigns where you have little information on targeting options. So if you found that the previous section that we discussed for developing a display campaign a bit cumbersome – you can use the Display Planner, in fact its recommended for beginners.

Like the Keyword Planner is used for Search Campaigns, the Display Planner is the tool used for developing Display campaigns on AdWords. The Display Planner provides detailed ideas for Keywords, Placements and all other GDN targeting methods to help you plan your display campaign.

The Display Planner also helps you estimate how your ideas can perform and historical costs, which will help you decide on bids and budgets.

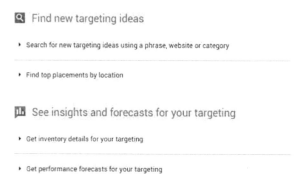

Creating Ads for the Display Campaign

It is easy to create ads for the Display campaigns. The text ads are very similar to the ones in Search Campaigns and can be setup easily.

The Image ads can be created by a designer or you can create an ad easily on the AdWords console by using the AdWords Ad creator – just provide your landing page URL and get ideas from Google on what your display ads can be. The format of these ads is HTML 5.

You can then select an idea based on its suitability and then customize the contents to your requirements.

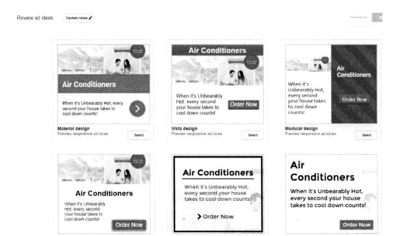

Once you have completed the development of ads, you can save them and the campaign will now be ready to go live. Congratulations - You Display Campaign is ready!

Chapter 7: Campaign Management and Campaign Optimization

Once your campaigns are running you can track their performance and optimize them to generate ROI and deliver better results.

7.1 Basic Metrics

Campaign Metrics

Metric	Explanation
Impressions	The number of times your ads have been served on the Google ad networks
Clicks	The number of times users clicked your ads
CTR	Click Through Rate = $\frac{Clicks}{Impressions}$ This metric helps understand the relevancy of your ad
Average CPC	The average cost per click
Cost	The total amount spent on your campaign
Average Position	This metric shows your ads position relative to those of other advertisers
Conversions	The total amount of conversions derived from this campaign
Converted Clicks	The total amount of clicks that turned into a conversion
Cost/Conversion	The average cost per conversion
Impression Share	The impressions you've received on the SERP network divided by the estimated number of impressions you are eligible to receive.

Illustration: Screenshot of the Campaigns Tab

Ad Performance Metrics

To view the ad performance metrics, you need to click the "**Ads**" tab.

Illustration: Screenshot of the Ads Tab

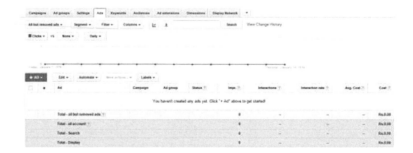

Keyword Performance Metrics

Illustration: Screenshot of the Keywords Tab

7.2 Performance Analysis

Performance analysis is the starting point for management and optimization of campaigns.

Segments

Segments Analysis goes a step further from your standard statistics and slices the data by time, click type or device. Here are a few insights that you can find when doing Segments Analysis:

1. Top Vs Others: Analyse how your ads are performing when they appear at higher ad positions versus lower ad positions. This gives you insights as to which is the best ad position for you.

2. Time: Analyse how your ads are performing at different times of the day, week, month, quarter or year. This gives you an idea on how to optimize your campaigns for the best hours or days of the week.

3. Click Type: Analyse how your ads are performing by where the potential customer clicked on the ads – headline, phone number, site-links, etc.

4. Device: Analyse how your ads are performing on different devices. This gives you an idea about consumer behaviour and device dynamics.

Illustration: Segments

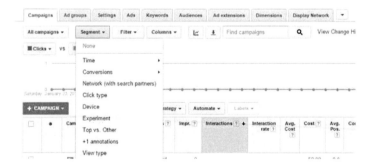

Dimensions

Dimensions lets you slice data similar to Segments – but on different parameters. Some of the key views available on the Dimensions tab are:

1. *Geographic and User Location*: In this view you can track where the clicks came from. The origin of clicks information can be used to refine the targeted locations.

2. *Time*: In this view you can track performance of your ads on an hourly basis and day of the week basis. This helps you in deciding on the hours and days for your Ad Scheduling.

3. *Destination URL*: In this landing page view you can track which webpages the clicks are landing on and how each of the landing pages are performing.

Illustration: Dimensions

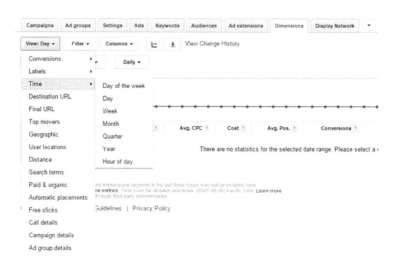

Keywords Performance Analysis

Keywords Performance Analysis can be done with three different tools:

1. General statistics available on the Keywords tab are available by clicking the Keywords Tab on the AdWords Console and shows you metrics like impressions, clicks, CTR, CPC, etc.

Illustration: Keywords Tab

2. Keyword Diagnosis Report available on the keywords tab by clicking on the Details tab and clicking the Keyword Diagnosis link and shows you whether your keywords are triggering your

ads and a snapshot of your keywords Quality
Score.

Illustration: Keyword Diagnosis

3. Search Terms Report is available on the
   Keywords Tab by clicking on the "**Search Terms**"
   button and shows you the keywords or phrases
   used by your prospects which triggered your ads
   and the performance metrics for those searches.
   You can use the search terms report to add new
   keywords which are not there in your campaign,
   add negative keywords which you don't want
   your ads to show for, refine match types of your
   keywords and provides insights for ad text / copy
   refinement based on what prospects were
   searching for exactly.

Illustration: Search Terms Report

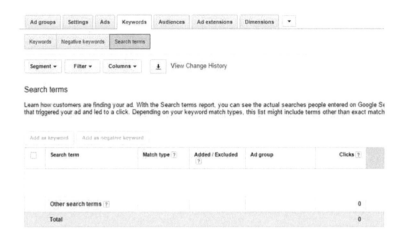

Ad Performance

Ad Performance Analysis enables you to see which of your ads performed well against the metrics like CTR, CPC, Avg. Pos. Conversions, etc. You can adjust the timeframe for viewing these metrics and also compare performance of two timeframes. Based on this you can pause the poorly performing ads and add new ads variations.

Illustration: Ad Performance

Sometimes the performance metrics can be too much to handle – in which case you can filter the required metrics through the Filter tool in the Ads tab. There you can use the filters to figure out which ads are delivering the highest revenues and profits, ads with higher Cost Per Conversion, etc.

Filter is very useful when you have a large account.

Illustration: Filter Ad Performance

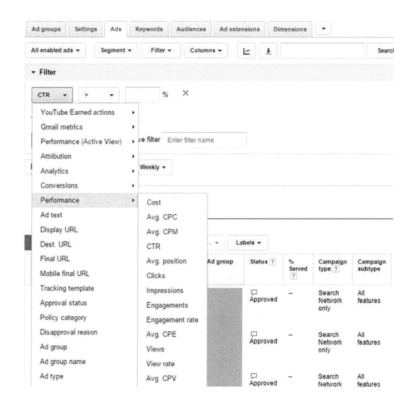

Ad Extensions Analysis provides you insights into how each of the ad extensions performed. This gives you insights into which extensions the potential customers are clicking — e.g.: if a particular site-link on prices is clicked more often, that means the customers are looking for prices and you can incorporate prices in the ad text to improve your ads' performance.

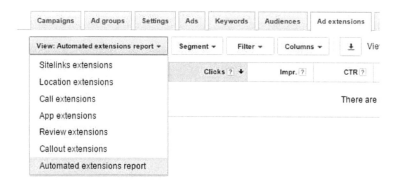

Top Movers Report

This report enables you to view campaigns that have the highest changes (increases or decreases) compared to the previous time period - in clicks, costs and conversions with an idea on what is causing it. This report gives you insights into which campaigns and ad groups you need to take action on and also see the impact of changes made previously.

Illustration: Top Movers Report

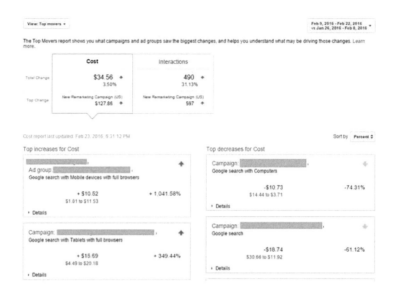

Auction Insights Report

Auction Insights Report provides you insights on your competition on AdWords for similar keywords that you are targeting and also some benchmarks on the performance against competitors. Auction Insights Report shows how often your ads rank higher than that of your competitors', share of impressions, avg. ad positions, campaign overlap %, ads appearing on top of page %, etc. These insights help you make decisions on keyword choices, bids and budgets by showing you where you are performing well and where there are opportunities for improving performance.

Illustration: Auction Insights Report

Auction insights report

See how successful your keywords, ad groups, or campaigns are compared to other advertisers participating in the same auctions.

19% of available impressions (from 8535 keywords) were used to generate this report. Learn more

Display url domain ?	Impression share ? ↓	Avg. position ?	Overlap rate ?
You	75.20%	2.8	--
	45.69%	5.2	53.69%
n	26.84%	4.7	30.53%
	21.29%	3.3	24.45%
com	16.89%	2.6	17.13%
n	16.11%	1.9	11.85%
	16.04%	2.5	13.92%
	15.70%	6.9	18.22%
com	15.06%	2.8	17.62%
.com	13.57%	4.7	13.46%
om	13.12%	4.5	10.30%
	11.94%	6.6	15.12%

7.3 Conversion Analysis

The most important performance measure or metric for any AdWords campaign is conversions. Conversions have to be measured against marketing or business goals for each of the campaigns.

If your marketing goal is sales or leads – you can measure them through Cost Per Conversion or Costs Per Lead, along with Number of Conversions and Conversion Rate.

If the marketing goal is Brand Awareness – you can measure it through Number of impressions, Reach and Frequency of Ads, and Customer Engagement.

7.4 Conversion Optimizer

Conversion Optimizer is an automatic tool that maximizes your conversions given your Cost Per Conversion (CPA) goals rather than focusing on Clicks (CPC) and Impressions (CPM). You can set the CPA to Max. CPA – the maximum you are willing to pay or Target CPA – the average cost you are willing to pay per conversion. To enable the Conversion Optimizer in any Campaign you should have had at least 15 conversions in the past 30 days.

Illustration: Conversion Optimizer

7.5 Analysis for Bid Adjustments

Bid Adjustments can be used to control when and where your ads are shown and to enhance the performance of campaigns, ad groups, ads and keywords that are working for you. We can make bid adjustments based on location, device and time.

Location Analysis and Location Based Bid Adjustment

Geo or Location based bid adjustment are increasing or decreasing bids for specific locations (countries, regions, states, and cities). This enables bid adjustments based on performance parameters for that specific location.

For example, If Kenai, Alaska is driving better conversions, you can increase bids for searches originating from Kenai. If Soldotna is poor in conversions, you can decrease bids for searches originating from Soldotna.

Illustration: Location Bid Adjustment

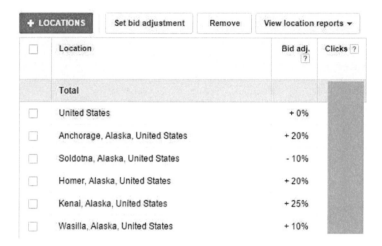

Device Analysis and Device based Bid Adjustment

Device based bid adjustment allows you to increase or reduce your bids for mobile devices. This enables you to target the potential customer on-the-go in a better way.

Illustration: Mobile Bid Adjustment

Device	Bid adj.	Clicks	Impr.	CTR	Avg. CPC	Cost	Avg. Pos.	Conversions
Computers		0	0	0.00%	$0.00	$0.00	0.0	0.00
Mobile devices with full browsers	+ 25%	0	0	0.00%	$0.00	$0.00	0.0	0.00
Tablets with full browsers		0	0	0.00%	$0.00	$0.00	0.0	0.00
Total - all experiments		0	0	0.00%	$0.00	$0.00	0.0	0.00
Total		0	0	0.00%	$0.00	$0.00	0.0	0.00

Time Analysis and Ad Scheduling Based Bid Adjustment

Ad Scheduling can be used to display ads in specific times of the day and days of the week. You can use bid adjustments with ad scheduling to increase or decrease the bids in order to improve the performance of your campaigns for specific parts of the day or days of the week.

Illustration: Ad Scheduling and Bid Adjustment

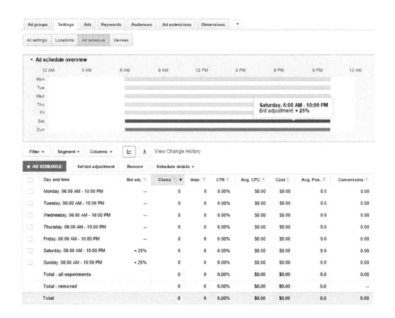

Quality Score Analysis

Quality Score is an aggregated estimate of your campaigns overall performance and measures the quality of your ads, keywords and landing pages. This shows you if your ads are relevant to your keywords, if your keywords are specific and not too generic in nature (measured by Expected Click Though Rate) and also if the landing page is responsive in design and provides a good user experience. Quality Score is rated from 1-10 where 1 is the lowest and 10 is the highest. By default, a Quality Score of 6 is given to a new keyword added to the campaign and later is changed based on the above criteria. It is always good to have your Quality Score to be 6 or higher.

Ad Rank is a measurement system that calculates a rank for all AdWords Accounts that are competing for a similar keyword. Ad Rank consists of Quality Score multiplied by the Max. Bid amount. The higher the ad rank - the higher ad position your ad will get and if the ad rank is lower than the number of ad slots available – then your ad may not be showed at all.

The higher the Quality Score the higher the Ad Rank you will get – resulting a higher ad position and your cost per click will be lower.

Ad Copy Testing

Ad Copy Testing or Split Testing of ads is an essential optimisation task. You can create different ad texts within the same ad group to see which one resonates well with the target customer and delivers better results.

The simplest way to test ad copy is having multiple ads with different ad copy running in the same ad group with the ad rotation set to evenly rotate. You can then evaluate the different ads on their performance like CTR, CPC, Conversions, etc. You can keep the better performing ads and introduce different ad copy based on the successful ones to optimise them further.

Another way to do this is turn on the ad rotation to optimise for conversions or optimise for clicks – this setting lets AdWords automatically optimise the ads that are performing better.

By optimising the ad copy – the performance of the campaign can be improved.

Impression Share Analysis

Impressions Share Analysis will give you an idea of the percentage of times your ads are showing based on all relevant searches that are there in the targeted locations of your campaign. So the closer the impression share is to 100% - means that your ads are showing to all the potential traffic on Google Networks.

There are separate metrics for Search Campaign Impression Share and Display Campaign Impression Share and both these can be accessed on the main campaign console of AdWords (if its not visible just go to columns and select the metrics to display).

There are 4 metrics within Impression Share Analysis – Impression Share, Exact Match Impression Share, Lost Impression Share (Rank) and Lost Impression Share (Budget). As explained earlier impression share is the main metric which indicates the percentage of times your ads are showing compared to a total possible. The other metrics support this main Impression Share Metric in providing more details.

Search Exact Match IS or Search Exact Match Impression Share show the % of queries that were matching the keywords in our targeting, this can be used to improve the keyword coverage from broad to phrase and exact match type. This metric is only for Search campaigns and not for display campaigns. All other metrics are available for both search and display separately.

Search Lost IS (Rank) or Search Lost Impression Share (Rank) is a metric which will show you the percentage of lost impression share due to poor ad rank – thus based on this metric you can improve the rank of your ads by increasing the bids, keyword mentions in the ad copy, and keyword grouping.

Search Lost IS (Budget) or Search Lost Impression Share (Budget) is a metric which will show you the percentage of lost impressions due to shortage of budget on the campaign.

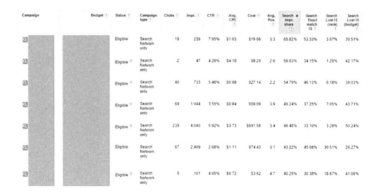

Chapter 8: Auditing your Google AdWords Campaigns Performance

Whether you manage your AdWords efforts in-house or outsource them to an agency, knowing how to audit the performance of the campaigns is critical. It's easy to get dazzled and even mislead if you do not align your campaign KPIs with your business objectives.

Make sure to evaluate how effective your AdWords efforts are in achieving your key business objectives by setting clear and relevant KPIs. The metrics should reflect what you would like to measure. When your campaign is targeted to generate online sales, the auditing is pretty straight forwards. You check compare the cost to the revenue and since everything occurs online it's easy to understand clearly.

Things get more complex when your campaign is targeted to generate offline sales.

Here are a few key metrics to evaluate:

Metric	Explanation
Clicks	The number of times users clicked your ads
CPC	Cost Per Click
Cost	The total amount spent on your campaign
Leads	Total number of leads generated from your campaign
CR	Conversion Rate from click → lead
CPL	Cost Per Lead $\frac{cost}{leads}$
SQL	Sales Qualified Leads – validated leads who have shown interest in the campaign product
Lead -> SQL CR	Conversion Rate from Lead → Sales Qualified Lead. This metric can help you evaluate the general quality of your leads. A good conversion rate indicates high quality leads. Whereas a low conversion rate indicates poor lead quality.
Customers	Total amount of new customers generated from your campaign
SQL -> Sale CR	Sales Qualified Leads → new customers. Used to evaluate the efficiency of the sales team.
Revenue	The direct revenue derived from the campaign
ROAS Rate	Return On Advertising Spent $\frac{Revenue}{Cost}$. This helps evaluate the overall profitability of the campaign and to evaluate the revenue generated for each dollar spent.

The best and most important KPI you can set for your campaign manager is ROI rate. Setting this KPI ensures that you get your desired return on investment.

The rule of thumb is to NEVER set your campaign KPIs by cost per click, impressions or leads.

Here's a quick example to prove this rule:

Let's take an example of a professional online marketing school who is trying to sell courses. Each course costs $1,000 and requires a graduate degree in order to enroll.

Campaign A

Keywords targeted — "PPC campaign management course for postgraduates"

Clicks	CPC	Amount Spent	Leads	CR	CPL	SQL	Lead -> SQL CR	Sales	SQL ->Sale CR	Revenue	ROAS Rate
100	10$	1,000$	20	20%	50$	10	50%	5	50%	5,000$	1/5

In this campaign each click costs $10 which sounds a lot for a $1,000 potential income.

However, this campaign targets highly relevant keywords that indicate that the user is more likely to convert, be eligible and eventually enroll.

We can see that the Conversion Rate from Click to Lead is high, the Conversion Rate from Lead to SQL is high and the Conversion Rate from SQL to Sales is high (the prospect knows what course he wants, and is a postgraduate); therefore, the Return on Advertising Spent (ROAS) from this campaign is 1/5.

The bottom line here is that for each $1 spent the company generates $5 revenue. Not bad!

Campaign B

Keywords targeted - "Online Advertising Courses"

Clicks	CPC	Amount Spent	Leads	CR	CPL	SQL	Lead -> SQL CR	Sales	SQL -> Sale CR	Revenue	ROAS Rate
1000	1$	1,000$	100	10%	10$	5	5%	1	50%	1,000$	1/1

In this campaign each click only costs $1 and each lead costs $10. Sounds good right? Look again.

This campaign targets broad terms that indicates that the user is not sure what he wants and might not even be eligible.

For those reasons the Conversion Rate from Click to Lead is lower than in campaign A, the Conversion Rate from Lead to SQL is very low and the Conversion Rate from SQL to Sale is low. (the person doesn't know what course he wants, and isn't necessarily a postgraduate) therefore the ROAS from this campaign is 1/1 which means that for each $1 spent the company generates $1 revenue. Not very impressive.

This example clearly amplifies why setting clicks or costs per clicks or leads as a KPI is wrong.

We see many companies who make the mistake of not analysing the data once a lead enters their CRM. This creates a blind spot for the company Google AdWords manager who can only set KPIs up to the level of cost per lead.

In such cases the AdWords manager does not have the relevant data to optimize campaigns for better ROI by learning which of the leads became customers and setting customers as a clear KPI.

How can you solve this? By getting sales and marketing on the same page otherwise known as Smarketing!

Smarketing

From Wikipedia, the free encyclopedia

Smarketing is the process of integrating the sales and marketing processes of a business. The objective is for the sales and marketing functions to have a common integrated approach This can lead to annual revenue growth of up to 20%, according to a study in 2010. The objective is to promote the product or service to potential buyers and at the same time integrate this process with the sales department's activities. Sales and marketing departments should meet frequently and agree on a common terminology, and using data throughout the entire sales and marketing process to identify good prospects and to follow up on how well they are followed up. Smarketing works best when a firm does closed loop reporting by tracking its success with particular prospects from the marketing stage through direct sales efforts. According to one source, Smarketing began around 2000 as a result of improved web browsing capabilities.

Getting sales and marketing aligned usually requires implementing several technological solutions.

Using a cloud based CRM that integrates with the media buying operation is usually enough on a technical level.

On a practical level, sales and marketing teams tend to not always like cooperating. We recommend implementing in-company regulations regarding workflows, lead scoring and updating the CRM about the sales that eventually occurred offline.

The key to success is to make sure your Google AdWords manager is well aware of your business objectives, and to ensure that you are measuring relevant metrics on your way to generating ROI. Low AdWords costs do not ensure sales. Be smarter, work as a team and use all the data you can generate to your optimization advantage.

Chapter 9: End Note – Rocking it

We hope that this book has helped you understand the role of Google AdWords in the internet advertising space. You should now have a fair idea of how to setup a search campaign and a display campaign and an understanding of campaign targeting, campaign structure, keywords, ad copy conversion tracking and of course, auditing and measuring ROI.

Remember that web marketing is constantly evolving. Make sure to channel your marketing efforts to platforms where you can track your progress and success and always check that you are getting the most out of your paid advertising.

We invite you to follow our blog at blog.boldigital.com for industry updates tips and special offers and welcome you to contact us if you have any questions comments or suggestions.

We wish you positive ROI and endless curiosity.

Good luck!

Bonus Chapter 10: Best Practices to Enhance Performance of your AdWords Campaigns

1. Frequently add negative keywords to cut wasted spends by irrelevant clicks.

2. Improve Quality Score to rank higher in Ad Position and pay lower CPC.

3. Increase your CTR by making your keywords and ads highly relevant to your target personas.

4. Have at least 3-5 ad variations per ad group – keep testing and improving.

5. Add long tail keywords (phrases with 2 words or more) which have lower CPC.

6. Improve Impression Share to reach more potential customers.

7. Have specifically designed landing pages for each ad group.

8. Add dedicated mobile ads and call extensions to target the customers on-the-go.

9. Add all Ad Extensions which improves CTRs and Quality Score.

10. Enable Conversion Tracking to track which keywords and ads drive profitable actions.

11. Micromanage bid adjustments (device / location / time).

Made in the USA
San Bernardino, CA
23 June 2016